CÓSMICA

A Poetic Journey to Awakening the Magic Within

A Collection of Poetry, Mantras and Magical Rituals
Natalie Garcia

CÓSMICA

A Poetic Journey to Awakening the Magic Within

A Collection of Poetry, Mantras and Magical Rituals
By Natalie Garcia

Natalie Garcia

Copyright © 2021 Cósmica.

All rights reserved. No part of this publication may be reproduced, distributed ut the prior written permission of the publisher, except in the case of brief quotations embodied in critical reviews and certain other noncommercial uses permitted by copyright law. For permission requests, write to the publisher, addressed "Attention: Permissions Coordinator," at the e-mail address below.

davina@alegriamagazine.com

Library of Congress Control Number: 2021921763
ISBN: 978-1-7379927-3-8

Published by Alegria Publishing
Layout by Sirenas Creative
Illustrator: Selina Saldivar

Dedications

*To all the women who believe in magic and love
with all their heart and soul.
You are proof that magic is real and that love
conquers all.*

*To all my friends & family, thank you for inspiring
and pushing me to write this book.*

To my daughter

Marley Sky, my baby girl; your light, and love are undeniable. Staying present and watching you grow into a wonderful human being is what life is all about, and I cherish every moment with you. Thank you for choosing me to be your mother. I love you a million times to the Moon and around the sun and back to Earth.

Trust yourself, remember you are a star, and shine bright everywhere you go!

Love you always,
Mom

Natalie Garcia

Dear Magical women,

We are living in a world that is full of contradictions and imbalances that can damage our overall well-being. What I learned so far from my experiences on this Earth and with others is that it's up to us to create stability within us first and find healthier ways to stay present to help us cope with unpredictable times. Everything else will align once we have a clear vision of our present moment. We don't need to constantly visualize the future and live-in fear of the unknown. We don't need to have a massive awakening to start living in the present, but instead, we can simply start by incorporating a walk, journaling, cooking a fun meal, or gardening into our lives. Staying present is a life-long goal that reminds us to stop and smell the roses as much as possible. With this book, I hope to be able to communicate and teach others to see the beauty in the world by appreciating the present moment. Living in the present is the only way to stay balanced between seizing the day and strategizing for a better future. It can be as easy as breathing in and out.

This book was created for all the women who supported my journey and showed me love and kindness along the way. This book was also created for the women who I didn't always see eye to eye and taught me about myself anyway. Lastly, this book is for the women who I don't even know, but who need love and support on their magical journey day to day.

Please remember and never forget you are brave, strong, powerful, and beautiful.

With gratitude y con mucho amor,
Natalia Garcia

Natalie Garcia

PREFACE

"Pursue the things you love doing, and then do them so well that people can't take their eyes off you."
- (Maya Angelou, I Know Why the Caged Bird Sings,1969).

As you open this book, I invite you to open your mind and heart as well. I believe that everyone's journey has a cosmic purpose and meaning. Cósmica is my awakened state of mind, a connection with my higher self and anything beyond this material world. It is a unique journey to awakening the magic within, as well as a journey of healing, and self-love. For me the connection with oneself is the most important one and it's always a never-ending journey. I had to let go of old views I was taught and did not connect directly with. I had to break away from the illusions and fears to reconnect with my authentic self and be able to speak my truth without shame or guilt of any judgement from anyone including my own. I realized I was the one creating obstacles for myself, and I was plagued with the stigma of mental illness after suffering a series of traumatic events through my childhood to adulthood. This book is my revelations of my own healing and self-love journey. I chose to no longer hide behind the mask of illusions and burdens not meant for me.

The process of writing this book was very intense and I had to look deep within myself to face all of me and my truth. I had to relive internally a lot of my own traumas from childhood to adulthood to learn to heal properly. These traumas didn't break me, but instead they made me more resilient and self-aware of my purpose. I was awakened to the reality of life and I could either be plagued by these traumas or I could move forward with love and strength for myself. Initially this book was supposed to be my road to self-care, but it became much more. This book is my freedom to say what I wanted to say, and I deserve to speak my truth. Instead of confronting, fighting, I instead gave it to God and the Universe. I am finally on a journey to understanding my own value and worth beyond every relationship I ever had including the one with myself.

Pain is something I know very well, but I did not want to be stuck in a cycle of victimizing myself. I wanted to break through my traumas and pain like the warrior I was born to be. I wrote this book to express my raw emotions, my feelings and my truth. I had a hard time accepting parts of my reality that were happening to me because they were pushing me to grow in uncomfortable ways. Deep down inside I'm an optimist and even in my darkest moments I try my best to see the light. As I wrote this book I was going through a lot of instability in my life. I lost my grandmother, I was overworking myself, I wasn't giving myself the proper love and I was going through a huge heartbreak. Writing it all helped me find clarity and I understood myself better through this journey. It is important for me to tell my story because as a woman I deserve to tell it and I want more women to tell their stories. I hope this book will inspire others to tell their truth and speak from their heart. With this book I share a lot of things I was avoiding and that I desperately needed to release. Anxiety has plagued most of my life and it often prevented me from moving towards amazing, but uncomfortable opportunities. I often fell victim to my own insecurities and doubts by creating obstacles that were not truly there. Sometimes we allow our anxiety to immobilize us, but we will never move past it if we don't face our fears that caused it in the first place.

Most often those fears are just illusions we've created in our minds because we are not comfortable with trying new things or facing the fears we hid away. So, I became my own test subject and the main research for this book. However, during my research I realized as humans, we are naturally trained to adapt to a new way of life and are searching for ways to persevere beyond the obstacles. Even though the light of joy flickers on and off it's important to find joy in all precious moments. Moments that we
often take for granted, like going for a walk, being able to write, read, dance or just move. Imagine being blinded by

your own traumas that you couldn't see the simple joys in our lives. Part of managing stress coping skills is also learning how necessary it is to keep our minds and home decluttered to reduce unwanted stresses. Keeping things clean and organized from your altar to your desk helps tremendously. Awareness and moving intentionally also helped me move past my moments of instability. Everything in this book from the mantras to magical rituals are things I have been doing for years to push through all the obstacles internally. One of my biggest inspirations is Maya Angelou because every single one of her poems speaks to my soul. However, it's the magic she radiated when she recited her poems that captivated me and it's like seeing a shooting star in the night sky. I was inspired by her natural ability to connect the energy of her words and engage her audience. Maya bravely stood up for the entire African American community and spoke out against the injustices and the oppression they faced. I hope to follow her footsteps and be a symbol of hope and healing for my own community and the next generation of women one day. With that being said, I welcome all to the magical world of Cosmica!

Natalie Garcia

AWARENESS

Natalie Garcia

GROUNDING RITUAL

Use this ritual to ease anxiety and ground you to the earth during panic attacks or social anxiety spells. This ritual is also great to do when you want to feel more connected to your ancestors and call on guides to help you with life's difficulties.

Intention
I am present
I am grounded in my power
I am deserving
I am whole

What you will need:
Palo Santo (cleansing)
Florida water or rose water
Sandalwood Incense
6 Small rocks or crystals that fit in the palm of your hands.
Quiet outdoor space
Floor pillow
Tobacco Scented Candle

Best time to do this ritual
Weekdays
Winter and Spring Season
New moon

Steps:
Cleanse yourself with palo santo
Spray Florida water or rose water on yourself
Sit outdoors in a quiet space
Light the candle and incense
Focus on your body's vibrations and the earth's energy
Feel the ground
Place 3 crystals in each hand and face palms up
Repeat mantras until you feel at ease
Breath 4 counts in and four counts out

Mantra:

I am here in the present.
Ancestors with gratitude I greet you.
I am grounded to the earth.

Deep in the shadows focus on the light

Natalie Garcia

THE ULTIMATE DESTINATION

Living, trying to avoid I'm asleep
Living, trying to forget I'm awake
Living, trying to find the answers to questions I can't say

Deep in the journey, it will be my ultimate destination

I ask for the truth... No lies
I ask for clarity... No illusion
I ask for forgiveness.... No fear

Deep within, it will be my ultimate destination

Looking behind in the past
Looking forward to the future
Looking here in the present

Deep in time, it will be my ultimate destination

Facing the reality, I can't escape
Facing the darkness, walking down the road
Facing the inevitable, everyone must go

Deep in the motion, it will be my ultimate destination

Without the dark, there is no light
Without the pain, there is no healing
Without the destruction, there is no rebirth

Deep in the tunnel of the shadows & light, it will be my ultimate destination

I was asleep, but now I'm fully awake
I was in fear, but now I'm at peace with no regret
I was anxious, but now I am content

Deep in the universe is my ultimate destination

{444}

Every ending is a new beginning
VIBRATE

I am connected through
CONSCIOUS

I dream it, I grow it
MANIFESTING POWERS

I live it, I love it
CO-CREATED

I am awakened
PURE ENERGY

I remain connected
CROWN CHAKRA

My spirit evolves
PHOENIX

My throne is within me
GODDESS

It's already written
CÓSMICA

Natalie Garcia

AWAKENED

I PROTECT MY ENERGY
The new me is stronger & free
Healing the whole family tree
It is meant to be
I am illuminated & connected to Mother Earth's frequency

The new me is in control for all to see
Healing myself with the Divine light and cosmic energy
This is exactly where I need to be
I am dreaming and living lucidly

The new me has awakened its memory
I am healed with prana moving inside of me
It is here, present where I shall be
I am connected reading all the signs and synchronicities

With my eyes closed, I observe within
With my heart, I attract all positivity
In this place of love and light, I shall be
I LET IT GO, WHAT IS NO LONGER SERVING ME

In the midst of chaos, you will find peace

BREATHE

The energy is always changing, stay present to see

FREQUENCY

Learn to love your storms and rainbows equally

GROUNDED

CHANNELING

My angels are talking to me
I'm not longer a part of this 3D
I'm not living a nightmare or a dream
I created my own reality
What do I see differently?
Love growing immensely
Invoking the goddess that has always been inside of me
I had an epiphany
I need to get out of my own way
and stop doubting myself and what I say
There's no one like me and fitting in is delusional
We are multidimensional
And we are all beautiful

Look in the mirror and repeat

Goddess mentality
The Cósmica inside of me
is awakening
Self-love is the key
I found emotional stability
No obstacle can stop me
I am on my own journey
I create the peace within me
I look around and see beauty
Most importantly, I see it inside of me

My angels are talking to me
They tell me to see the beauty of the world through me
Look beyond what the ego wants me to see
There's nothing outside but illusions
Don't judge, we are just humans
What does it all mean?
The message is you are a queen
Stop questioning
Start manifesting

To women awakening the magic within,
remember we came here to win

Look in the mirror and repeat

Goddess mentality
The Cósmica inside of me is awakening
Self-love is the key
I found emotional stability
Nothing is stopping me
This is my journey
I create the peace within me
I look around and see beauty
Most importantly, I know it's inside of me

Write your own mantra...

Natalie Garcia

CREATIVITY

Natalie Garcia

CREATIVE MUSE RITUAL

Be your own creative muse and awaken your creative senses with this ritual. This special creative ritual focuses on awakening the creative muse within and allowing your ideas to flow out. Most importantly this ritual will help start manifesting and putting those ideas in motion.

Intention:
I am awakening all of me
I am the muse and feminine divine of my own life
I am open to new possibilities
I love me

What you will need:
Sage
Rosemary Incense
Notebook
Pen
Cósmica Candle
Rosewater

Best time to do this ritual
- Wednesdays
- Anytime you feel a creatively blocked
- Waxing Moon

Steps:
1. Connect with your higher self by asking
2. cleanse your space with sage
3. Light the Cosmica candle and Rosemary incense
4. Breathe in and repeat the mantras
5. Meditate for 10 minutes
6. Visualize your muse and your creative self-connecting with you
7. For 10 minutes write down your thoughts and ideas that come to you
8. Keep doing this ritual daily for the entirety of the waxing moon until the new moon

Mantra:
I speak freely
I think clearly
I feel authentically
I am creatively free

Write your own mantra...

I surrender to the universe willingly
I surrender whole heartedly
I surrender to free myself from the stagnant energy
I surrender with trust & love

BREATHE AND RELEASE

Rushing through life is mindless
Leaving you constantly breathless
Remember there's a skill in stillness
Breathe & Release
Relax and put your mind at ease
We are connected through nature's frequency
Mother nature is in you and me
Breathe in life and energy
It's constantly moving inside poetically
Surrender and see
You are breathing your own mantras and poetry

Natalie Garcia

THE DAUGHTER, THE MOTHER AND THE EARTH

All women are daughters
All women come from mothers
We were made from the cosmic colors

She was born from the energy of the **SUN**
The **MOON** illuminates her divine path
The **STARS** guide her to her destiny
The **EARTH** calls on her and connects her to the ancestors
The **WIND** awakens her powers
The **OCEAN & SALT** protect her unconditionally
She cultivates **LOVE & LIGHT** within
She remembers she's the daughter of the Great Spirit
GOD is inside her
Born and reborn for the universal balance
Let go of all fears
The journey was made for LOVE
Let go of all guilt
The journey was co-created by GOD

All women are daughters
All women come from mothers
We were made from the Earth for one another

FEMININE DIVINE

Trust her
She is brave
Dealing with emotions that are not hers

Understand her
She is strong
Handling the pain that is not hers

Help her
She is powerful
Fighting battles that are not hers

Tell her
She is beautiful
Channeling love and light in her

Respect her
She is wise
Manifesting a world outside of her

Protect her
She is connected
Creating life and cosmic energy within her

Love her
She is untainted by the material
Loving purely & unconditionally above her

ENERGY FLOW

Our soul is our ego
We nourished it with love
PRANA
LOVE in the heart
LOVE on the mind
GOD BLESSED
No competition, no negativity, no fear...
ROOT CHAKRA
We set the trend
SACRAL CHAKRA
We connect within to ascend
SOLAR PLEXUS
We evolve with no end
REBIRTH
We say the mantra
OM
We feel it... **HEART CHAKRA**
We hear it... **THROAT CHAKRA**
We see it... **THIRD EYE**
BALANCED
Filled with peace, love & light
CROWN CHAKRA
We've been sent here with love and purpose
DIVINE
We are connected through all the motion
COSMIC ENERGY
Final stage is clarity
TRANSCEND

DREAMER

I am from here and there
I am the daughter of the earth
I am the mother of my descendants
I am the dreams of my indigenous ancestors
I am the spirit of the jaguar hunting in the jungle
I am the mermaid swimming in the sea
I am the roses growing beautifully with thorns
I am the hummingbird flying in search of freedom
I'm proud, I'm a fighter, and I'm a dreamer
I am from here from this ancestral land
That calls me with its energy
I am from my parents and my grandparents a
Their land running through my veins
I'm from the spirit of love
I am and always will be
I am here to stay
I am from here and there

LA BRUJITA DEL JARDÍN

La brujita dances to the flicker of the candlelight
Under the Luna llena, she mediates
She feels amor, luz y energía
Hechizos and magic, she cultivates

En el jardín corta hojas de Aloe vera for eternal beauty
She picks Lavender to relax the body & pensamientos
She brews Yerba buena te' to clear the anxiety
Sage and ruda are used for protection de las
malas vibras and for healing

La brujita escribe mantras, y poemas
She heals, nurtures, and breaks free
Under the sun, she manifests and co-creates
Love and light, she radiates

En jardin she uses black tourmaline for grounding energy
Rose quartz for self-love and positivity
On her finger, she wears an opal stone ring to
stimulate creativity
Aquamarine removes the blocks of verbal
expression for individuality

La brujita del jardín gives thanks and gratitude
Amor y paz para las abuelas y madres
She walks the path de sus antepasados
With love, humility & an open heart,
she connects & illuminates

COSMIC CONSCIOUSNESS

THERE IS NO BETTER TIME THAN HERE TODAY
To feel the emotions and illuminate
Breathe in **INTENTION** and meditate
Connect & feel yourself go all the way

To connect and elevate
Dream, **TRANSCEND** and activate
Travel through space, just fly away

THERE IS NO BETTER TIME THAN HERE TODAY
To heal darkness and feel renewed
Surrender to **STILLNESS** and give gratitude
Project love, light, and forgiveness every day

To quiet the ego and find wholeness
Connect with Self, **ALIGN** and gain awareness
Accept the mind-body-spirit is one, don't allow it to stray

To find balance and stability
Redirect your energy and **EXPAND** positivity
Visualize love and cosmic energy coming your showering you in every way

THERE IS NO BETTER TIME THAN HERE TODAY
To find peace within
Awaken my inner **DIVINE** in a harmonious way
Deep in the shadows focus on the light, this is the only way

To unite and manifest
Feel the bliss to **EVOLVE** and radiate
Listen to your Higher Self and co-create each day

Write your own mantra...

_____

_____

_____

_____

_____

_____

_____

_____

_____

_____

_____

_____

_____

_____

_____

_____

NOPALERA

They call me la nopalera
I grow wildly in the desert fields
With flowers y espinas
Soy la nopalera
It's a symbol of my legacy
I wear it en la frente para que todos los sepan
La sangre Michoacana siempre corre por mis venas
Barefoot I walk to connect to this indigenous land
A land I've known for many lifetimes
Me llaman la nopalera y nunca se me olvido
El apodo nunca me ofendido
I embrace las raíces de nopal
Soy como mis abuelas y las abuelas de ellas
Con un gran honor
Es mi sello de amor y valor
Soy la nopalera
Y lo digo con mucho orgullo

Natalie Garcia

EMPOWERMENT

Natalie Garcia

I manifest under the moonlight
    But this good fortune is my birthright

Write your own mantra...

_____

_____

_____

_____

_____

_____

_____

_____

_____

_____

_____

_____

_____

_____

_____

_____

Soy de Aquí y de Allá

Soy la hija de la tierra

Soy la madre de mis descendientes

Soy los sueños de mis antepasados indígenas

Soy el espíritu del jaguar cazando en la selva

Soy la sirena nadando en el mar

Soy las rosas creciendo bellas con espinas

Soy el colibrí volando en buscas de libertad

Soy orgullosa, soy una luchadora, y una soñadora

Soy de aquí de esta tierra ancestral

Que me llama con su energía

Soy de mis padres y de mis abuelos

De sus tierras que corren por mis venas

Soy del espíritu de amor

Soy y siempre seré y no me voy a ir

Soy de aquí y de allá

COSMIC GODDESS

The Moon, the Sun, and the stars are aligning
I stand in the power of my fertility
Manifesting and giving birth to my new beginning
I stand balanced and within me there is stability

In my reflection, I speak the words from my heart
Cósmica soy y tu eres
La diosa te dio todos tus poderes
Diosa soy y tu eres
Tonantzin vive entre de todas las mujeres
Divina soy y tu eres
Madre Tierra te da el control de todos tus placeres

The Earth, the wind, and the seas come together through energetic frequency
I stand in my power of Divinity
Manifesting and giving birth to the new me
I am continuously healing by channeling my Goddess energy
I stand and connect with the higher me
I embrace the Goddess within me

In my reflection, I see a divine work of art
My Cosmic Energy
Flourishes from every part of me
My Goddess Energy
Radiates from inside me
My Feminine Divine energy
Cultivates within me

The higher me, my feminine divinity and my cosmic energy are connecting
I am a Goddess channeling new possibilities
Everything is aligning for me
I found my new stability
I have the power of fertility
I nurture and grow my abilities
I reflect pure and cosmic energy back to me

MY POWER

I am not who you think I should be
I am me
Your trauma can no longer affect me
I pray for you and me
You were the best parents that you could be
Given your circumstances and our family history
I am grateful for what you gave and did for me
But your negativity will not be passed on to me
I stopped this cycle, and it will not repeat within me
Your fears can no longer traumatize me
I will change the traditions of misogyny
I'm aligned with my ancestor's teachings and spirituality
So, I can continue to walk the path that God claimed for me
To be who I want to be
I move forward in abundance and positivity
I cut the cords to the traumas that immobilized me
I choose to parent my daughter differently
I am best mother I know I can be
I am who I want to be
I walk with the light within me
No one's negativity will ever harm me
I speak these words in GOD's harmony
I know who I want to be
I am the brave woman I grew to be
Your thoughts and actions will no longer affect me
You have no power over me

To the ex-lovers who once said they loved me
I am not the person you think you see
You had no right to violate me
You manipulated me
You tricked me
You projected your jealousy and insecurities onto me
You shamed me
For what I wanted to be
You said you loved and cared for me
You lied continuously

Cósmica

You had no loyalty
You never laid a hand on me
But your words were abuse to me
Stop yelling at me
Stop talking down to me
Stop pretending you are loving me
You had no right to isolate me
This is not love to me
I disconnect from this karmic energy between you and me
I am not the naive 21-year-old girl you think you see
That is no longer me
I am not the words you say to me
Your abuse will not affect my child or me
I learned the lessons this relationship taught me
I am healing tremendously
I walked in gratitude and GOD upgraded me
I grew to love me
I love myself truly and endlessly
Your words no longer exist within me
You have no power over me
I walk with love within me
No one's words will every harm me
My thoughts flow within harmony
I know who I want to be
I am the strong woman I was built to be
I stand up for my children and me
Your thoughts and words will no longer affect me
You have no power over me

To the negative people around me
Who are you to tell me, who I should be?
You do not get to label me
I am who I chose to be
I am bigger than what you see
You don't get to categorize me
I am multi-dimensional and infinite energy
Your perspective does not affect me
You are free to see what you want to see
But don't try to make me believe that is the real me

I see the real me
Whispers and opinions never bothered me
That's you depleting all your good energy
Your evil eye and jealousy will never affect me
And before you come for me
Walk very cautiously
Know your negativity
Will come to back to you and not to me
I will continue to live optimistically
I see the world I want to see
Your negativity will never affect me
I live abundantly
Not focused on material and money
But love, inner peace, and cosmic energy
This is my energy, and no one can take it for me
I walk with magic within me
No one will ever harm me
With their dark negativity
God is always protecting me
My Ancestors are guiding me
The entire Universe is behind me
I am connected and in harmony
I am the powerful woman I was made to be
I stand up for my children and me
I let go of the everything no longer serving me
I release all this negative energy
I co-create the only good energy
I manifest what I want and see
This what you call Alchemy
I am reclaiming the power within me

Write your own mantra...

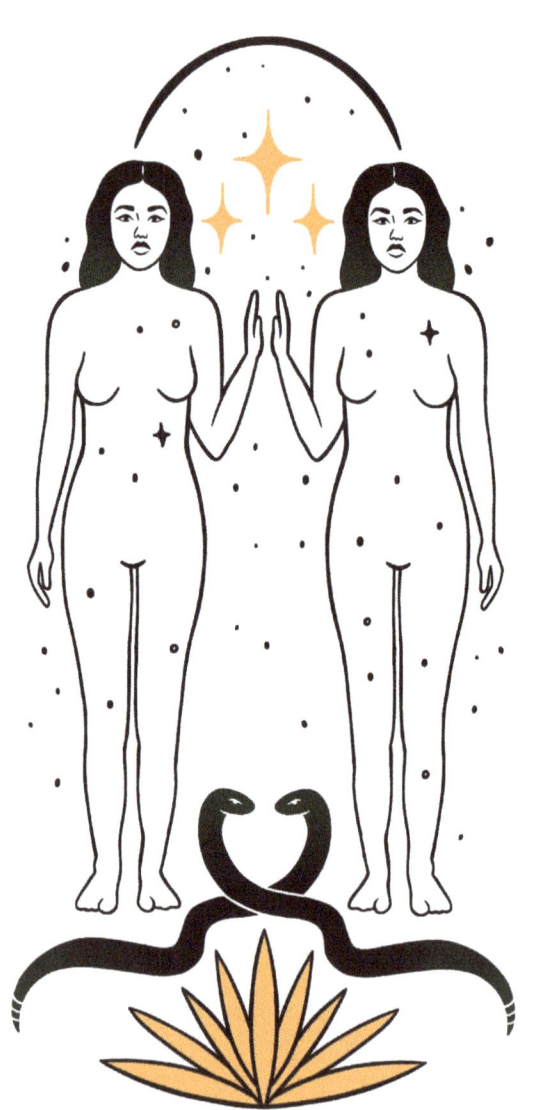

MAGIA DE MUJER

When the sun sets
The magic of my soul connects and resets
I breathe in amor y prosperidad
These are the moments I fall deeply in love with myself y lo que es la belleza de mi realidad

I am no longer chasing the idea of perfection
Every night, I rest with gratitude in my heart for a deeper connection
I love myself complemente y sin complejos
Tú eres magia mujer y se lo digo a todos los espejos

I will not apologize for giving myself the love I deserve
This is how I surrender and embrace the beauty of the universe
Estoy sanando los corazones rotos de mi madre y de mis abuelas
I stand in my magic y bailo abajo de las estrellas

When the sun rises
The magic of my body awakens and stabilizes
I breathe in a new day of gratitude and abundance
These are the moments I feel alive again and grateful for my ancestor's guidance

Natalie Garcia

WOMAN/MUJER

I'm a WOMAN with my own story
There's nothing yet written in history
But I am quite extraordinary
I'm multi-dimensional and infinite energy
I walk with love & strength inside me
I'm a daughter
I'm a mother
I'm a sister

I'm a WOMAN and I'm creating my own story
My individuality is my poetry
I'm healing and I am a healer
I'm a student and teacher
I'm the change and the stability
I am the fight and the tranquility

I'm a WOMAN and this is my story
My gender will never define my glory
I am inspired and inspirational
I can be soft and unbreakable
I am confident and vulnerable
I stand alone and I'm capable
I stand with my sisters, and I am unstoppable

Write your own mantra...

CHICANA

100% Chicana
Tengo sangre Indigena y soy pura Michoacana
Nunca me senti 100% Americana
Pa' nada
Las gringas dicen que soy más bruja que santa
Yo me río porque su miedo me encanta
Es pura ignorancia
No, les tomo nada de importancia
Yo me amo y me querio como un tesoro
Y con mucho orgullo me pongo mis coquetas y medallas de oro

100% Chicana
And I say it with pride
I refuse to assimilate and hide
I'm from here and from over there
I speak loud Spanglish while moving my hands in the air
You can try to imitate if you dare
But watch me break down the stereotypical walls
And throw you couple hechizos and crystals balls
F*ck your racist obstacles
I walk with my ancestors and spirit guides above all
They told me to take up space and not make myself small
I'm educated, I'm humble, but I will dance circles around you
Smiling and calculating the next potion to brew
Sí, soy bruja, I'm a goddess and I've been since the womb
MAKE WAY! MAKE ROOM!
I am not asking for permission
I'm flying on my high on my broom

Did you hear me clearly?
Soy 100% Chicana from Cali
Representing the San Fernando Valley
Valley Girl, but don't confuse me with a white girl named Kendall or Kylie

I only drink pura tequila Mexicana
"Then go back to your country!"
¿Qué? WHERE?
Mi pasaporte dice Americana
I'm not going anywhere
I'm the daughter of immigrants with native blood
I grew like a lotus from the sacred mud
Soy Mexicana y Americana
I'm 100% Chicana

I'm brave
I'm strong
&
I'm powerful

Soy valiente
Soy fuerte
y
Soy poderosa

Natalie Garcia

UNCONDITIONAL LOVE

Natalie Garcia

UNCONDITIONAL LOVE RITUAL

Unconditional Self-love is the key to prosperity and to living freely. Learning to love and accept yourself during the dark moments on your journey will open a world of possibilities. This ritual will give you the love to pamper yourself through your journey.

Intention
I love myself unconditionally

What you will need:
Rose petals (pink petals to represent unconditional love)
Himalayan Salt ½ cup
Epsom salt ½ cup
Rose Incense
Rose oil
4 Pink candle

Best time to do this ritual
- New Moon
- Full Moon
- Friday, Saturday, and Sunday
- Fall Season

Steps:
1. Run a warm bath
2. Light Rose incense and candles
3. Pour salt, rose petals, and rose oil in the bath
4. Breathe and visual yourself covered in love
5. Focus on the love within
6. Breathe 7 counts in and 7 counts (repeat 3x's)
7. Say mantras out loud

Mantra:
I am embarking on my journey of self-love
It's a journey of pure unconditional love
I love myself truly and purely throughout my journey

Cósmica

I am ready to embark on my self-love journey
I am open to the possibilities of love
I am open to the experience of love
I am here to love
I am ready to receive love
I am love

THE LOVE CHILD

All she ever wanted was something so real and unconditional
The hopes of love awakened her every day
She wanted to feel like nothing she had ever felt before
The fire burned inside her for more and more

She makes everything an adventure
Because her inner child never went away
She endures so much and survives it all
This is why her parents built her this way

Even though the unknown terrified and thrilled her in many ways
She yearned to create something
Magical and enchanting inside her
The emotions made her connect with herself every single day
But she never let go of morals or traditions
Despite her wild rebellious ways

She questioned the existence of divine timing
Deep inside she knew the universe always worked in mysterious ways
The most precious thing she owned was her pure heart and energy
This is why she was made this way

She doesn't want to be a prisoner to herself
She observes and laughs at her mistakes
She apologized for her pride, but never for her compassion
Or even the human contradictions that make up her DNA

She knows in this material world nothing lasts forever
In her dreams, it does so she meditates every day
Until it manifests and becomes real one day
This is why she vibrates love every single day

THE LOVE JOURNEY

You make me feel like those love songs I hear on repeat
My heart dances, and my mind is constantly daydreaming
Thoughts of you make me smile and visualize a never-ending future

Is this love?

You make me feel like I am swinging with my eyes closed
My heart races, and my mind spins with no control
The laughter and joy drown out the sound of all my sorrow

Am I falling in love?

You make me feel like every day is an adventure
My heart is on another frequency,
and my mind is full of energy
We are connected and grow organically

Did I fall in love?

You make me feel like nothing I have ever felt before
My heart is open, and my mind is free from any worries
Trust, respect, and loyalty I pledge for eternity

This is love.

You make me feel like I do not want this to ever end
My heart will shatter, and my mind will never forget
I promise to never take you for granted because I love you more every day

I fell in love.

Cósmica

You make me feel like I want to grow our family
My heart explodes, and my mind plays tricks on me
My emotions remind me to live and enjoy every present moment

I'm in love.

You make me feel exactly how I prayed to feel
My heart loves you purely and my mind is at peace
Thank you for loving me so unconditionally
I love you always on this journey....

Natalie Garcia

The journey won't be easy, but I will grow and love who I am becoming every day.

Natalie Garcia

THE TWIN FLAME JOURNEY

Neither of us were looking for love during our solo excursion
Stagnant water from the past created doubt and confusion
But there's no denying
This is divine timing
For all the lessons to start aligning
We fell in love unexpectedly in every way
We submerged into each other all the way
Together we were meant to sail
And this journey is nothing like an ordinary fairytale

We battled many emotional tides of uncertainty
Yet our love is meant for eternity
Perfection doesn't exist on this journey
We will crash into many waves during our quest
We must learn many lessons in order to progress
Our voyage outlasts forever
It is more than just a foolish love letter
Love and faults can't be measured to move forward for the better

Deep down we know this is a different love ship
We are more than just a failed sunken relationship
Because you are the sound of the tranquil ocean waves
I am the love storm your heart connects with like music and sound waves
Nothing can compare to our courageous journey
God gave us endless possibilities and we are worthy

You say, "Realistically, these love stories never last"
Remember, I am an extraordinary woman incomparable to all the mermaids from your past
We are not a predictable love story
We are an unbelievable twin flame journey
Brilliantly embarking and sailing through our own creative odyssey
Exploring our telepathic connection and poetic intimacy
You and I will always be the epitome
Of true love beyond this reality

CÓSMICA MANTRA

I Ignite and breathe in intention
I meditate and love my reflection
I bathe in the light of self-love and confidence
I am the Cosmic goddess
I manifest & let it grow
I breathe & go with the flow

COSMIC WOLF

Come home soon
My body is howling at the moon
Let's submerge in poetic intimacy
Read me line by line
Fall down the rabbit hole and enter my cosmic divine
Write your name on me
I belong to you unconditionally
Kiss me cover to cover
There is another world for you to discover
Read me over and over
I wrote this message for you to secretly uncover
Mi amor, come home soon
 I promise I will make you howl at the moon
Let's become one with the celestial gods
Fulfill the prophecy written in the stars
Euphorically dance in the 5th dimension
Let's align and surrender to our cosmic connection
Explode in ecstasy through our mystical ascension
Hear my call, this our souls' intention

SENSUALIDAD CÓSMICA

I've been waiting for you on this journey
Can you feel my energy calling?
Come to me

Close your eyes and feel my cosmic sensuality
Dance and vibrate with me
Discover me

Sensualidad cósmica
Abreme de pierna a pierna consume me como
una historia erótica
Spread my legs
Open me

Taste my supernova and kiss me slowly
Devour me passionately
Awaken me

Take me to the moon with you
Make me feel brand new
Explore me

Land on every galaxy inside of me
Set the cosmic goddess free
Desire me

Nuestra conexión se magnifica
Y me convierto en tu diosa cósmica
Transform with me

Your musical notes are spiritual codes
That illuminates my darkest roads
Enlighten me

I am your ethereal beauty tonight
Connecting with your internal light
Unite with me

Make me yours on this cosmic journey
I'm devoted to you unconditionally
Claim me

THE HEARTBREAKING JOURNEY

I couldn't find the courage to say goodbye
I couldn't find the words to tell you I was hurting inside
I couldn't repeat myself again & say "I want to spend more time with you"
I couldn't tell you that I was giving up hope waiting for you
I couldn't destroy the beautiful vision of one day having your child and marrying you
I couldn't hear you tell me I was being irrational, and this wasn't going to work for you
I couldn't bear to think you might replace me with another woman who doesn't even know you
I couldn't face the truth that our journey was ending, and I was going to be without you
I will always hold on to the love manifested between you and me that made us once happy
And maybe I'll see you on our next journey.....

MOTHER O SHORE

You are the sun of the family
Full of grace and love for all
Radiating eternal sunshine for all

Time taught you lessons
Time gave you betrayal
Time broke open your heart
Time tested your faith and devotion
Time showed you how truly human we ALL are

You are the heart of the family
Suffering quietly from heartbreak, rejection and neglection from all
Loving unconditionally through it all

Time teaches you how truly powerful you are
Time always reveals the truth
Time gives you wisdom and courage
Time allows you to heal and recover
Time shows you to love yourself above all

You are the oracle of the family
Glowing with love and light from above
Blooming like a beautiful rose with thorns from below

Time is truly the lesson
Time is your connection to God
Time reveals to you the universe is always on your side
Time shows you to move with your head high
Time allows you to grow and evolve your heart's desires
Time is what we create to learn how worthy of love we all truly are

Love is the connection
Have faith one day you will find
the steady tide
Love is the reflection
Embraced all the emotions inside
Walk your true prophecy
Love is the resiliency

SINK OR SURRENDER

I'm not good at saying goodbye
I want to pretend you are still traveling and working
By now, you would think it would be easy for me to accept your absence
We were always so close and infinitely connected
But why did you feel so cold and distant sometimes?

Maybe I'll heal and move on
Maybe I'll dwell and regret it all
Maybe I'll cry until I drown in an ocean filled with my own tears

I don't want to say goodbye
I want to believe we will still work out
By now, you would think I'd be jaded by my string of multiple heartbreaks
We always said we would be there for each other
But why did I feel so alone?

Maybe I'll rise like the phoenix and let go
Maybe I'll pretend I'm not bitter and broken from another failed relationship
Maybe I'll meet someone else who will never compare

I can't say goodbye
I want to visualize our love can conquer it all
By now, you would think I'd see things more realistically than optimistically
I blamed the women from your past for your lack of emotions and cautiousness
But why did you pick me after being broken by them?

Maybe I'll fly like the cosmic wolf and embrace
my newfound freedom
Maybe I'll question if you ever truly loved me and die alone
Maybe I'll just give up on love once and for all
But I am still here in love with myself

THE REBIRTH JOURNEY

UNSPOKEN

I have so many questions
So many feelings
I can already feel you pulling away from me
There's an agonizing feeling
Should I be leaving?
Say something
We can't keep internalizing everything
Your silence is scaring me
I'm overthinking
I can't keep pretending
There's something you are not telling me
Every unspoken word is killing me
I'm in this relationship by myself
And it's unfair to me

SPIRALING AND QUESTIONING

Lost in assumptions and thoughts of betrayal
Triggered by the past and an unknown future
Exposing my emotional patterns & traumas
Your distance planted seeds of self-doubt
I doubt if I'm worthy
Abandoned by love, this is fucking hurting
I feel defeated on this journey
I don't know where I'm going
Did you truly love me?
Or did you just want to conquer me?
Everything is now a question to me
Lack of communication gave me no hope and no understanding
What's the truth anymore? I can't think clearly
I'm drowning in my own confusion slowly

DEATH

Submerged and cleansed by my tears
With acceptance and exposed fears
That part me of that loved you endlessly
She's no longer here
She's resting in peace
This heartache was her end
We both lost a rare woman, a good one, a true friend
Dearly beloved we mourn a great loss
The one that called you beautiful and handsome when you doubted yourself
The one that cooked and served you at midnight when you were hungry
The one that massaged & rubbed your hands when you were tired and overworked
The one who loved you unconditionally for just being you
My condolences, mate
I grew.
That part that wanted to connect with you deeply
now carries a different tune and frequency
Wish me well
Keep me in your thoughts and prayers
Because I am now more self-aware
I deserve more than promises full of dead air
I need a real connection
Love without restrictions
No holding back and no limitations
No false hope, no modifications
Loving hard and moving forward through all the complications

REFLECTION

Truthfully, you should've been more aware
Your heart was broken before me and that wasn't fair
You deserved genuine love & someone to truly be there

God answered your prayer
I was chosen to be there
To remind you that hearts like ours need to be handled with care
And love comes with a sincere responsibility
Because broken hearts can be emotionally deadly
Just look at me
Once an optimist, I thought we were meant to be
And this was going to be a different story
Realistically, you will forever miss me
You will forever think of me
Hopefully, you remember me in all my loving glory

RESURRECTION

I resurrected the strength in me
The faith in me
The hope in me
The love in me
I forgive you and me
I turned these lessons into clarity
Trust and communication are the key
I accept all of me
I'm evolving
I'm growing
With LOVE inside of me
LOVE for my heart's journey
I know I will always be worthy
And you don't fucking deserve me

Natalie Garcia

Amid a broken heart and grief
I found peace
I fell in love with me
I love myself even when I am happy, sad,
angry, cheerful, and lonely
This is when I connect the most with me
When I stop neglecting who I am truly
I understand me
I feel the emotions inside me
I see the light and the darkness within me
I love me
Unconditionally

Brokenhearted
Healing
Glowing
Shining
Pivoting

SHADOW WORK

Natalie Garcia

MIRROR CONFIDENCE RITUAL

This ritual was created to install confidence while we are going through shadow work. Sometimes shadow work can deplete our confidence and overwhelm us with emotions. This ritual is focused on building resilience and bravery to keep going on the journey with a major energy push.

Intention:
I reflect love and confidence back to me

What you will need:
Mirror
White rose petals
Sandalwood incense
White candle
Jasmine essential oil

Best time to do this ritual:
Anytime needed

Steps:
1. Light white candle and incense
2. Sprinkle rose petals all over your altar or around the space you are doing this ritual
3. Sprinkle Jasmine essential oil on the candle
4. Look at yourself in the mirror and say the mantras below
5. Meditate for 10 mins in front of the mirror with your eyes closed
6. Repeat the mantras in your head or to yourself

Mantra:
I stand in my power of confidence
I am brave, strong, and powerful
Good fortune is my birthright

HUMILITY

The state of humbleness

Where pride, ego, and judgment do not exist.

The lessons of humility are the hardest to see

But come with the biggest blessings.

Embracing the Shadows

I've been fighting it all-day
Pride and hate have no say
I forgive you, ego, you were weak,
Find the wholeness and patience you seek

I've been in my thoughts all-day
Fear and darkness go away
I forgive you, mind, you were lost
Find the peace at all cost

I've been avoiding it all-day
Pain and sickness cannot stay
I forgive you, body, you had no escape
Find the love and healing to reshape

I've been speaking all-day
Nonsense and dishonor steer away
I forgive you, ancestors for writing it this way
I will find my guidance and stillness today

I've been seeking all-day
Answers to the questions I cannot say
I forgive those who yet don't know
Find the balance and the glow

I've been struggling all-day
Negativity and confusion breakaway
I forgive me, I am human, and it will not always be this way
I accept my mistakes and let them go away

I face my shadows here today
Gratitude and forgiveness let me find my way
I am a part of you like you are a part of me
We are connected as one everyday

Behind Pain Lies Strength

Behind the smile, there's a pain
A pain you think no one will ever understand
Pain that seems too hard to look far beyond
But this pain isn't a punishment
Pain and joy are as natural as night and day

Behind the pain, there's strength and resiliency
There are moments where you find your stillness
These moments are filled with gratitude and appreciation
These moments make you realize that pain is a part of your journey

Behind the strength and resiliency, there's love
Love for yourself
Love for your journey
Love for others
Love for all the moments
Love for the darkness and the light

MY FRIEND UNTIL THE END

La Muerte, she's a dear friend
She was the only friend there when my life almost ended
As I nearly drowned at 5 years old
She whispered "Look up and grab ahold"
Close to my last breath, I coughed, and then she let go
I'm grateful I was allowed to live and continue to grow
Since then, she's someone I closely know

La Muerta, she's a real and true friend
She's consistent and a godsend
I always know when she's near
And soon she will be coming here
My abuelita has been waiting for her, patiently
I hope when it's her time, she leaves peacefully

La Muerte, she's a loyal and trustworthy friend
I know that she will be here until the very end
I asked her to explain life and death to me
Death is a confusing and different type of energy
I am deeply afraid, I must confess
There's so much more I can't process
Why must everything end?
She whispered, "It must always end because, this how you ascend"

La Muerte, she's truly a kind friend
Her strength and grace are a gift given to me to comprehend
There are no guarantees except for her visit at the end
She's the light and darkness I will always defend
Her beauty is something I truly commend
La Muerte, she's a very good and loyal friend
Rich or poor, strong, or weak when there's nothing left to pretend
She, too, will become your best friend
If not now, then eventually at the very end

NATALIE CARDONA DE VALDIVIA

Fue Hija, Esposa, Madre
Abuela y Bisabuela
Y como mujer nunca será olvidada
Fue hija de Refugio y Josephina Arambula Cardona
Nunca conoció el descanso ni como niña o ni soltera
Pero hoy, descansa en paz y tranquila
Fue esposa de José Valdivia
Para ella el matrimonio era su mayor sacrificio
Pero hoy, sus sacrificios son por vencidos
Fue Madre de once hijos
Maria
Felicitas
Teddy
Lola
Rosa
Jose
Salvador
Maria De Jesus
Juan Carlos
Consuelo
Y Estela
A todo los amo de diferentes maneras
A nadie los querías más o menos ni primeras
Y con este último adios, se despide de todos iguales porque ella no más vino de pasajera
Fue Abuela y Bisabuela
De nientos que la conocieron de lejos
Y de nietas rebeldes, pero con morales y tradiciones
Pero hoy quiere que la recuerden como realidad era
Era mágica, humilde, pensativa, inteligente, admirable y sencilla
La amargura de la vida nunca la consumió
Ella canta cuando nadie la miraba
Ella habla dormida
Aplaudía y le gusta recordarse de los tiempos pasados
Ella pasó sus últimos meses de no olvidarse de su familia
Ella rezaba siempre por nosotros

Fue una gran mujer
Porque su familia survivor pobrezas, hambres y batallas
Ella le dio vida a una generación
De Luchadoras, guerreras, y viguerías
Y esas mujeres y hombres le dieron vida a otra generación nueva
De artistas, maestros y consejeros
Somos una familia hecha de la luz de una mujer maravilla
Y hoy nos despedimos de una gran mujer
NATALIA CARDONA DE VALDIVIA

Write your own mantra...

The Empath Mantra

I feel my emotions today
I will not runaway
I observe them, it's the only way
I allow myself to breathe and rest every day

I am strong
I am brave
I am powerful
I am beautiful

I accept the emotions I feel today
I breathe in and set my intention every day
I am loved in every way
I exhale and release it away
I give gratitude and love to myself especially today

I am love
I am blessed
I am restored
I am balanced

WORST OF ME

You showed me a mirror of me
I saw the good, the bad & the ugly
Yet you still loved me
I never felt more like me & free
I never felt ashamed of my own negative energy
Yet you still loved me
You were there when I couldn't do it anymore
You reminded me of the strength I had inside to soar
I don't care if you know the truth about me
Sometimes I act as if I don't even need you and I rather be free
But the truth is I am never felt freer and more like me
You bring out the best and worst in me

ACCOUNTABILITY

Where should I start
My broken heart?
Why do I do this to myself?
I neglect me
I avoid my needs and never express myself freely
I need to stop projecting my fears and insecurities
I should stop fighting the lessons that I need to learn within me
I cannot let my emotions consume me

You showed me a mirror of me
I saw the good, the bad, and the ugly
Yet, you still loved me
I never felt more like me and free
I never felt more ashamed of my own negative energy

All I wanted was to hear was let's just focus on you and me
Let's be the partners we were meant to be
But the universe showed us you needed to focus on you, and I needed to focus on me
Profound journeys are never easy
I wanted to write our vows, not our eulogy
Here I am mourning and grieving
You will never be my enemy
Even with this chapter ending our love will never be dead to me
All I wanted was for you to love me relentlessly
But we let our fears come between you and me
We were consumed by uncertainty
We were not living realistically
Please know, I did love you unconditionally
And I'll take accountability

I will no longer neglect me

I will no longer avoid my needs and I will express myself freely

I will not repeat the same patterns of the old me

I surrender to learn the lessons within me

TRANSPARENCY

I see you, darkness
You came to me early
Through death, violence
rape, self-destruction, and toxicity

I feel you, loneliness
You were channeled within me
Through neglect, grief,
Anger, despair, and lack of intimacy

I understand you, hopelessness
You were created so effortlessly
Through self-sabotage, trauma, persecution,
Betrayal and insecurity.

I hear you, sadness
You are always there even when I am smiling
You were manifested through aggression, frustration
depression,
avoidance and fragility.

I taste you, bitterness
You are a recipe made from what was passed on to me
You were rooted in me through fear, humiliation, rejection
resentment
Shame and lack of vulnerability.

Write your own mantra...

SURRENDER

In all transparency, I battle with PTSD, depression, and anxiety
You will never see it by just looking and talking to me
I became good at hiding and pretending
Superwomen like me cannot be weak or break easily
It created a void inside of me
I am filling it with my writing and poetry

I am healing slowly
But it is a daily struggle that chokes me
Flight, fight, and fear - I feel it constantly
I have shadows that haunt me
I tried to avoid them until they almost drowned me
This is me, authentically

I am not weak, I am not fighting, I surrender freely
I create my own reality
My empathy is a gift God gave to me purposefully
This is my vulnerability and humility speaking
I move with my intuition and the power inside of me
I breathe deeply
With gratitude, I release everything no longer serving me

DARK CONSEQUENCES

I sabotaged myself once again
I repeated my old patterns
I lost myself and doubted who I am
I was confused
I shed tears I couldn't hold back in public
Memories flooded my mind
Pain consumed my heart
This is what being truly broken feels like
My biggest fear came to life
I sabotaged myself once again
I lost myself on this journey
I am aware now what I didn't know then
I forgive myself
I hope you forgive me too

DESERVING

You deserve every piece of me
Back, hand, and head massages

You deserve home cooked meals and dessert
Three to four entrees

You deserve unconditional love
I love you always on this journey

You deserve peace and serenity
I kiss you gently all over and whisper I love you

You deserve to be who you are freely
I laugh at your jokes and commentary

You deserve every inch of me
I am yours always, take me

Except, during giving you what you deserve,
I neglected what I deserved
I neglected my own feelings
I suppressed my wants and desires of having my own family
I allowed the years to pass by organically without telling you
what I needed to be happy
I neglected to see you were not ready for me
I was in denial and too proud to admit it was the wrong timing
I put my emotions last and never made them a priority
I couldn't tell you the truth, I feel so lonely
I neglected what was inside of me
I neglected what I deserve to feel happy
I am re-writing my story and there's no need to say sorry
I needed to learn this lesson for my own clarity and
understanding
I am just as deserving
I am worthy

LIVE LEARN AND LET GO

I let go of the past
I let go of all the memories good & bad
I let go of all the false hope
I let go of all the visions that never became a reality
I let go of all the hurt
I let go of all the regret
I let go of all the mistakes I made
I let go of all the moments of confusion
I let go of all the miscommunication
I let go of all the doubt
I let go of being impatient
I let go of being frustrated
I let go of the resentment
I let go of the fear
I let go of the sadness
I let go of the anger
I let go of the glimpses of what you & I could've been
I let go of the pain
I let go of the heart break
I let go of all the unsaid things
I let go of the grief
I let you go
I let us go
I let go with love in my heart
I let go with peace in soul
I let go wishing you joy & happiness
I let go praying for your blessings & well-being
I let go knowing I tried my best at the time
I let go knowing I loved you completely
I let go because I loved you unconditionally
I let go because I love myself more
I let go freely
I let go to find a new beginning
I let go but you are forgiven
I let go but I forgive my myself
I let go to heal this broken heart
I let go because I still want to believe love conquers all

I let go because I deserve peace
I let go because I deserve to truly be loved the way I deserve
I let go because I deserve stability
I let go because I deserve certainty
I let go because I deserve balance
I let go because I deserve consistency
I let go because I deserve the opportunity for unity
I let go because this burden is too heavy
I let go because I speak to God daily
I let go because I want to feel love expand
I let go because I want to grow
I let go because I want real love to never let me go
I let go because I want a better future
I let go of everything no longer serving me

Natalie Garcia

GRATITUDE

Natalie Garcia

Don't let the visions of a future that has not happened yet blind you to the joy in the present time.

You are in the right place
at the right time.

Natalie Garcia

SELF TRIUMPHS DOUBT

Self triumphs doubt all day
When you learn to believe it
Honor it

Self destroys doubt everyday
When you learn to spread your wings and fly high
Believe it

Self drowns out doubt any day
When you learn to love the journey and run with it
Love it

Self-doubt is not a weakness
Self can triumph over doubt all day
Self can destroy doubt everyday
Self can drown out doubt any day

INTUITION OVER MIND

I sit in my solitude until I find my peace
Plagued by the veil of illusions that I need to release
I sit in the obscurity of my discomfort to find the light of contentment
I release the darkness of all my fears and resentment

Intuition over mind
I am more powerful than these fears and insecurities I create and find
I am human and I am full of contradictions
I am a woman perfectly created from natural imperfections
I bask in my internal cosmic light
I release, surrender and no longer fight

I no longer hide from my fears and the insanity of my humanity
I sit and face the shadows haunting me
My truth will always set me free
I sit and overcome the loneliness I created in my mind
Deep in my internal chaos, I will remain aligned

Intuition over mind
I leave this battle of my emotions and traumas behind
I sit in the power of my higher self to bring me peace
I am connected and creating my new legacy
I sit in my stillness and embrace my serenity
I am the reflection of my own peaceful reality

La Soñadora

Nunca soltó sus morales y su tradición
A pesar de sus caminos rebeldes y salvajes
Se disculpó por su orgullo,
pero nunca por su compasión y contradicciones humanas
Que componen su ADN
Porque soñaba con crear un mundo tan mágico y real que la despierta
día tras día....

MARLEY SKY

Angelita
You were born from a wish and a star
Astrologically birthed from the fire of sun
Cosmically created from God's delight
Look at you
You are a shooting star
Never forget how magical you are
I love you my little butterfly
If you ever have a doubt look up to the pink sky
And spread your wings and fly

REST IN GRATITUDE

With a mind full of thoughts
I can't remember when I heard silence in the dark
Talking to myself, trying to connect the dots
Regretting mistakes and thinking of every remark
Remembering old conflicts
Stressing about imaginary new ones
None of these scenarios truly exist
But it's taking a toll on my body and spirit like a ton of bricks
I am unbalancing my mind with this endless list
Focused my breath, I say the words of my inner Alchemist

I sit in gratitude
I give gratitude
I honor my gratitude
I am gratitude
I speak gratitude
I observe in gratitude
I connect with gratitude

From above my head to the ground below
I allow myself to reset and let go
I disconnect from theworld I know
I am no longer looking at the future show
My present is where I will continue to grow
I allow mind to go with the flow
As I breathe in and say the words below

I sit in gratitude
I give gratitude
I honor my gratitude
I am gratitude
I speak gratitude
I observe in gratitude
I connect with gratitude

I am no longer stressed
My body will rest
My mind will let go of all signs of distress
My soul is at its best
I lay down with one last deep breath and rest
In gratitude
I feel healed and completely renewed

INVOKING PEACE

I call upon my higher-self and divine light
El angelito de mi guarda
Walk me through this emotional and fearful fight
Protégeme con tu amor y poderosa espada
Allow me to step forward and grow
Con mi fuerza y valor
Allow me to focus on my highest purpose and harvest the seeds of abundance I sow
Dame los poderes para vencer este descontrol
With your reassurance and guidance, I flourish
Dame la seguridad de salir por delante con la energía del sol
Release me from these limiting beliefs and fill me with purpose and courage
Mi Angelito de mi guarda siempre, eres mi dulce compañia y mi calma
Thank you for walking with me on this journey
Con mucho amor y paz en mi alma
Your royal blue light is always with me
Angelito, gracias a ti
I feel at peace and completely free

MASCULINE DIVINE

Hombre estatua
Eres el dios del agua
You are the epitome of beauty
Your scent is strong and sweet like the Earth
Your body is steady and powerful like the ocean
Your touch and kisses awaken me

Hombre bello
Caistes del cielo
I submerge in your love
With every deep stroke
I connect with your frequency
You ignite the elements within me

Hombre divino
Eres un genio
Your soul is pure and gentle
Your emotions flow like water
Your silence is your power
Your thoughts are your gifts
Channel the energy within

Write your own mantra...

BAILANDO

Yo bailo, I dance
Bailo y bailo para olvidar las tristezas del mundo
I dance and dance y respiro profundo
Yo soy la ballerina y bailó con Pachamama
Bailo y bailo para liberar mi alma

Yo bailo, I dance
When I feel sad, anxious, and fearful
I dance to connect and feel once again spiritual
Yo bailo until find my breath
I dance and dance from birth until death

Yo bailo, I dance
I dance to inspire otros que aman y bailen también
I dance and dance to see the beauty in my world again
Yo soy el colibrí bailando bajo del cielo rosado
Bailo y bailo hasta que mis preocupaciones han pasado

Yo bailo y bailo
Respiro
Y me voy de paseo
I breathe
 let go
I dance with the flow

OPTIMISTIC TEARS

I don't go into relationships searching for red flags
I wear my heart on my sleeve
Always
I love from deep within
Always
I don't know if there's something wrong with me
Or the rest of the world
Somehow, I always end up with tears
Lessons to learn and grow from
Saying goodbye with pain
Telling myself, "Remember to stay gracious and move forward."
I'm strong and I can walk alone
But I yearn to connect with the one
Feeling shorted and dismissed
I still have hope

These are optimistic tears falling down my face
I cry with grace
I love wholeheartedly even when I know I am going to fall
I can't be mad at myself for risking it all
Love is always worth it
Heartbreak is humbling
Teaching me lessons and newfound clarity

I don't leave relationships searching for another one
I love too hard and immensely
My connection doesn't break so easily
I know there's plenty of fish in the sea
You don't have to keep telling me
I know I should keep swimming
But I'm tired of drowning in uncertainty
I want stability and security
I want unconditional love not fake displays
I've overcome many thunderstorms and tidal waves

But I now yearn for grounding and tranquility
Feeling disappointed and defeated
I still have faith

My optimistic tears cleanse me
I cry until I'm free
My emotions are the power within me
I am growing and evolving
Learning my lessons and turning them into clarity
I am falling in love with myself and my journey

Write your own mantra...

Trust the process
Observe
Enjoy the journey
Reflect
Dance with love
Breathe
You are the co-creator

ABUNDANCE

Natalie Garcia

ABUNDANCE RITUAL

This ritual is focused on abundance and removing any lacking thoughts that no longer serve you. When you are in the mindset of lacking your vibration is low. Abundance is like the air you breathe, the water you drink and the force of life within you. You are never lacking when your vibrations and your mindset is focused on abundance.

Intention:
I am abundance
I am whole
I am connected

What you will need:
Bowl
Salt
Fresh Spearmint
Broom
Green or white candle
Rose incense

Best time to do this ritual:
- Friday morning or night
- During the waning moon
- Spring season

Steps:
1. Fill the bowl halfway with water
2. Pour salt into the bowl
3. Light your candle and put it in the bowl
4. Cut the spearmint with our hands and sprinkle it in the candle and salt water
5. Focus on breathing in and out
6. Meditate 10 minutes on abundance flowing inside you and all around you
7. With the broom sweep out any negative energy in your area
8. Focus on abundance growing continuously

Mantra:
Abundance flows and moves within me always

I am abundance and it moves and flows
always within me

WITHIN ME

I look up, I see Abundance

The world and the sky are filled with many wonders
I see the beauty in all
Even when I am in despair and my tears fall
I see magic everywhere I go
Even when I feel radiant or completely low
I see the power of love and I know abundance will overflow

I look up, I feel Abundance

I don't search for it at all
It's the energy inside me and I feel its call
Even in the moments of confusion and doubt
I surrender by dancing, singing, and crying it out
I feel secure and connected
Even in the moments of solitude or when I feel tormented
I feel the peace in my stillness
I feel the light of my darkness

I look up, I am Abundance

The power of love and gratitude block all fear
Even when they tell me I don't belong here
I look up, stand proud and tall
I allow the Universe to take the lead when they wish for my downfall
I look up, this materialistic world is not the only world I know
I am grounded with gratitude as I continue to grow and grow
I channel abundance everywhere I go

Write your own mantra...

Growth is love

Your growth isn't only about the flowers blossoming.

Your growth is also the seeds, thorns, weeds, and the dry patches.

Self-love is loving yourself entirely; even on the days your growth is uncomfortable.

Love is growth.

MADRE

Mujer estatua
La piel morena y con las pecas de bronce
Con tu silencio inciendistes la noche
La luna y las estrellas nacieron de ti
Mujer cósmica
La bruja de honor
Eres la madrina de la astrología y los cometas
Con tus relámpagos de amor illuminates el sol y los planetas
Mujer maravilla
Divina tú eres entre el mar y la tierra
Caminas como un tornado en el desierto
Con la pasión y la belleza de una encantadora tormenta
Mujer bendita
La Tapatia con sangre india
Sagrado es tu vientre cósmico
Con tu sonrisa le distes vida al universo
Madre mia
Soy la hija de la luz hecha de tu energía Cargo el valor y la humildes de nuestro linaje
Y tú cósmica esencia
Gracias por darme los poderes de diosa
Y por mi existencia

RECLAIMING THE FAMILY TREE

I wake up the family tree
I am the child of the divine
I am the first generation to break the cycle of pain
I am proud and I say it loud
I come from a beautiful HERITAGE full of love, full of culture, and history

We came from warriors, fearless leaders, and cosmic beings
We came from the generations of courageous heroes
We came from the Natives of this sacred land
We came from the ancient Aboriginal womb
We bleed blood with DNA embedded from the motherland

You tried to make us forget but we remember
You yell "Go back to your country"
You know our roots are planted here
Your violence will only make us stronger and more united
Your wall will not stop us because we learned to fly
Your laws will not destroy us or break us
Your hate will not win over our love

I pray to my ancestors whose blood is shed all over this land
I will continue to uplift and fight for the people you take for granted every day
I am my ancestor's manifestations and dreams
I am rebellious and I will go against the status quo
I am powerful and I can do anything I set my mind to
I am brilliant and I will always succeed
I am a spiritual warrior, and I was born to soar

We are protected by God
We will continue to invoke our magic inside
We will heal ourselves generation after generation
We will heal the entire family tree

I am the child of the divine and have awakened the tribe inside me

CONVERSATIONS WITH THE MOON

Querida Luna
At night, I pray to you
Manifesting my dreams and wishing they'll come true
I see the reflection of me
Opportunities, insecurities, duality, and purity
It's my sign to focus and embrace the new me
I take full accountability
To heal and create a new peaceful reality
I allow divine time to flow naturally
To feel the emotions and set myself free
I will not ignore what was inside me
I cannot suppress my needs and dreams
I will no longer please others so freely

I need loyalty
I give myself the loyalty I need
I need transparency
I give myself transparency
I need honesty
I give myself honesty
I bathe in the magic of the moon

I continue to expand infinitely
I understand the stagnant energy was distracting me
From discovering my worth & capabilities
I am making myself a priority
Giving myself more love on this journey
I deserve love without fear, doubt, and uncertainty
I birth a new cycle of peace and stability

HEALING
8.28

When cycles repeat
I am healing
I observe my feelings
I honor myself, I love myself, I take care of myself
I deserve to heal
I am healing
I pick myself up
I exist and this is my journey
Cycles are meant to be broken
This is healing
I am focused on my healing

Through my feelings

Write your own mantra...

INFINITELY ME

Soy La Brujita del Jardín
I am the feeler of energy
The manifestations of the creator dancing freely
I was made differently
Born more aware and revolutionary
Prophetic dreams connect me to another realm and reality
Gifted so ravingly with visions of the past and future
I bloom like a metaphysical rose embracing my painful thorns
Always with a bit of humor
Channeling messages and connecting with the ancestors
"No fear, no attachments, we are only visitors"
Childhood trauma invoked this magic within me
I am not here to harm anybody
That's why the moon and the sun have always guided me
Protected and cosmically connected
The sweet Earth and the animals talk to me energetically
La brujita nació dentro de mi
Para nunca estar sola and that's the way it was supposed to be
This path was destined for me

I am the rebellious daughter | La rebelde
The outspoken one
I speak my mind and don't think twice
No, I will not join the sorority or the fashion club
I like hanging out with the misfits and the underdogs
Soy la malcriada for not following the rules
I can do whatever men do, watch me
No, me voy casar porque me dices que ya es tiempo
Si con mucho respeto but don't try me
I have a way with words that will bring the most egotistical men to tears
I know truth and mirrors are their biggest fears
I dance on edge of danger just to feel a rush of freedom
The destroyer my family calls me
While I say fuck misogyny
La niña fuerte y salvaje and that is the way God intended it to be

Soy la madre soltera | The single mother I chose this path
Mejor sola que mal acompañada
Better alone than with bad company

You've heard that story
I chose this path intentionally for my daughter and me
I had to leave to break free
She deserves a mother who lives authentically just like me
Healing and feeling
Even if it's just her and me
I chose this unconventional path mostly for me
No lying
No gaslighting
No verbal and emotional abuse
No codependency
One day, my daughter will understand me
Why I chose this difficult path so wisely
I am honoring the little girl inside of me
Even if sometimes I feel lonely
I refuse to settle for a man who doesn't truly value me
Or pretend I am religiously married and Instagram happy
For the sake of what? A dysfunctional family!
No, not me
I cut the cords to all the cycles not meant for me
I am the woman who walks alone courageously
The she-wolf hunting and hustling
Until I find a lone wolf who runs free just like me
I chose this path to learn to love all of me and that is why I walk with goddess energy

I am Cósmica
Infinite energy
La Diosa caminando con los rayos del sol
Confident y Segura
Naked and free
Hair long like the sea
Dancing with the moonlight
Soy feliz
No se nada y siento todo
I am the goddess of love and fertility
The essence of simplicity and creativity
I am just me
No words are necessary
I am created by the cosmic energy
The entity of who I am truly

Awakened and loving purely
This is my journey to living authentically
And this is how the magic is created within me

Natalie Garcia

Self-Love is Abundance
I love myself more
I honor myself first
I do not lose love
I gain love

WITH GRACE AND BEAUTY

One thing you should know
The universe is always on my side
I cultivate love and purity from within never seeking it on the outside
I love unconditionally from every place inside of me

Watch me grow and flourish endlessly
Every flower blooming is me
Every plant growing organically is me
Mother nature is all of me
I am the breeze
I am the sea
I am the stars and moon shining brightly
I am the warmth you feel, but don't see
I am the love you miss daily

I am the craving you feel constantly
But your guilt and shame won't let you reach out to me
I am the woman you will seek in fantasy
But those facades and mermaids will never be me
They will never compare to me
I am on another frequency
You need to learn all the lessons of humility
Until then I am everywhere and everything is me

You can always feel me
Everything reminds you of me. Why? You ask
The Universe wants you to always remember me
That's now your reality, there is no turning away or escaping
I am the magical woman you manifested before you were ready
But you neglected to truly see me and love me when you had me
I trust the Universe will reveal to you who I am truly
And you will never forget me

DAY BY DAY

I am focused on myself
I am focused on my healing
I am focused on my self-love journey
I am focused

CONNECTED

Natalie Garcia

ELEMENTS CONNECTION RITUAL

The elements (water, air, fire, & earth) are great ways to invoke the power within ourselves. We have a great deal of energy and we can all invoke all the elements inside us to help us connect with our higher self and gain inner prosperity. Use this ritual to connect with the element and awaken the magic within. This ritual intensifies your manifesting powers.

Intention:
Invoke the elements and connect with my higher self

What you will need:
Green candle (Earth)
Red candle (Fire)
White Candle (Air)
Blue candle (Water)
Mirror
A glass of water or Florida water
White rose or carnation
Rose incense or favorite incense

Best time to do this ritual:
- End of the season: Spring, Summer, Fall or Winter
- Full moon
- Can do this ritual naked

Steps:
1. Light all four candles and place them in a circle around you
2. Sprinkle water on the white flower
3. Use the flower to cleanse your energy from head to toe
4. Recite the mantras below
5. Dance in a circle and kiss the mirror
6. Meditate for 10 minutes

Mantra:
Feel the positive energy grow
Feel the energy within
Feel the energy all around
Feel the energy protect me

Feel the energy

POSITIVE

Feel the energy all around

AFFIRMATIVE

Feel the energy within

INTUITIVE

Feel the energy connect

RELATIVE

Feel the energy grow

ELEMENT

AUGUST 28

Astrologically birthed from the fire of Mercury
Took my first breath at 3:16 AM and open my eyes with curiosity
Gifted with numerologically
Gifted with prophecy
Created in the womb from magic, trauma, and tragedy
Born a witch destined to invoke magic practically
Genius with spells and bruja craft
my words are magic, I see the future and your past

Nació la Brujita Cosmica
Tengo el alma de diosa
Con el corazón lleno de amor pero bien furiosa
No tengo nada de Cristiana
La piel de gitana
Muevo mi caderas de Mexicana

Behold
Alchemist turning ideas into gold
I channel my ancestors and spiritual warriors
No need for followers
It's a lonely road
I travel alone
Astrologically birthed from the moon of Aquarius
My coming of age is glorious
Cosmically connected and always protected, victorious

ARIES

Born to fight, love and repent
Restored
You are the phoenix rising as one
Stand with love
There's no end
No pride
Vulnerability will lead you to ascend

TAURUS

Grounded with strength
For your loved ones you will go to great lengths
Bounded to loyalty and resilience
Connected through experience
Your heart will be your greatest defense
Let go of the fear and move on with brilliance

Natalie Garcia

GEMINI

Forward thinking
Ever changing chameleon
You dance with the stars and float in air
Focus on yourself and become more self-aware
Let go of what you can't control
And never be ashamed of your multidimensional soul

CANCER

The loving one
Break down your wall
The caring one
Show your true emotions once and for all
The loyal one
Flow with vulnerability and you will never fall
The strong one
Listen to your heart's call
The inspirational one
Express your true feelings and stand tall

LEO

You are the golden light that radiates
Walk, talk, and open all the gates
Leaders like you are astrologically born and made
You have the power to teach those who are not afraid
Use your gifts to help those around you unconditionally
Blessings come when you are selfless completely

VIRGO

You are keeper of simplicity and abundance
Move to the front with grace and confidence
Modesty and shyness will fill you with regret
Pursue the opportunities you deserved but are too fearful to go get
The universe is calling you to something new
Stay true to you
Embrace your imperfections, it's the power in you
It is time take a chance on you
Make all your wishes come true

LIBRA

You walk with a deep sense of understanding
Balancing the scales and always expanding
Blessed with many open roads and paths to take every day
Move with love every step of the way
Observe and learn the lessons of humility
Breathe and release the indecisiveness that leads you to immobility
Your honest word will shatter any obstacles with agility
Influence comes from honesty and credibility

SCORPIO

The warrior of light and dark
You dance on the edge, a true Joan of Arc
Speak with truth and pure intentions
Your abilities come the steady flow of emotions
Confidence and bravery will open every single door
It's written in the stars you are meant to fly and soar

SAGITTARIUS

A true heroine and dragon releasing fire energy
Breathe and count to three
Choose to write your own story
Don't chase those who will never understand you
Hold your head high with every force inside of you
Bridges must burn to remove stagnant challenges
New chapters are created to restore the balances

CAPRICORN

The leader of the family tree
Always grounded to reality
Do whatever brings you peace
Your honor and integrity will never cease
Close your eyes and manifest your dreams
You come from a long line of kings and queens
Don't forget so easily
You will continue the legacy

AQUARIUS

With strength and curiosity
You think beyond this reality
Your metaphysical connection is your freedom
Leading the cosmic wolf pack every season
The chosen trailblazer of the new renaissance and spiritual realm
You are here to lead, not solve everyone's problems
Stay true to your majestic philosophy
There's always more for you to learn on this never-ending journey

PISCES

You are the essence of the ocean
Waves of love and commotion
Embrace your solitude
Peace comes from gratitude
Look within to feel connected and renewed

The Universal Purpose

The purpose is to **CONNECT**

The connection is to **ALIGN**

The alignment is to **EVOLVE**

The evolution is its **PURPOSE**

11:11

Natalie Garica
Poet, Writer and Creative Director

Natalie Garcia is a Los Angeles-born Chicana poet, writer, and creative director. Natalie has worked with many top-tier clients and brands. Her innovative strategies and campaigns have garnered media placements on CNN, New York Times, Washington Post, BuzzFeed, Cosmopolitan, Seventeen Magazine, PopSugar, Refinery29, LA Times, and more.

Natalie's writing focuses on self-love, healing, and spiritual practices. Her first book "Cósmica" is a collection of Spanglish poems, mantras, and magical self-care rituals. It will be published in the fall of 2021 with Alegria Publishing. Natalie is currently pursuing her Ph.D. in Positive Psychology to help normalize therapy, brujeria, and trauma healing in the BIPOC community.

About Illustrator

Selina Saldivar
Illustrator, Lettering Artist, Designer

@ayselinita | ayselinita.com

Selina Saldivar is a Chicana lettering artist and illustrator who is based in Houston, Texas and the Rio Grande Valley. She worked as in-house designer for corporate companies across the US for almost decade before pivoting to a full-time career in lettering and illustration. Selina has been a guest on Adobe Live, and her work has been featured across social media by Goodtype, Procreate, Coca-Cola and more. She loves to create illustrations that include positive affirmations and bold female figures. Her artwork is inspired by social change, mental health issues, self-love and empowerment.